Tom Thumb

Adapted by Sheila Lane and Marion Kemp

Illustrations by David Anstey

Take Part Starters
Level 2

Ward Lock Educational

Ward Lock Educational Co. Ltd.
T.R. House
Christopher Road
East Grinstead
RH19 3BT

A member of the Ling Kee Group
London · Hong Kong · New York · Singapore

This adaptation published 1989
© Sheila Lane and Marion Kemp
ISBN 0 7062 5118 0

All rights reserved. No part of this publication may
be reproduced, stored in a retrieval system, or
transmitted, in any form or by any means,
electronic, mechanical, photocoping, recording or
otherwise, without the prior permission of
Ward Lock Educational Co. Ltd.

Printed in Hong Kong.

Contents

1 **The Thumb Family**

2 **Tom in the Horse's Ear**

3 **Tom and the Robbers**

4 **The Thumb Family Again**

★ This sign means that you can make the sounds which go with the story.

The Thumb Family

In this part of the story you will read about:

Mr Thumb,

Mrs Thumb,

and Tom Thumb, who is no bigger than his father's thumb.

Mr and Mrs Thumb are measuring Tom to see if he has grown.

Mr Thumb Don't stand on your toes, Tom!

Tom I'm not standing on my toes.

Mr Thumb Yes, you are! Hold his heels down, mother! Now, Tom! Stand up tall.

Mrs Thumb Stand up tall, Tom.

Tom I AM standing up tall. Well . . . have I grown a bit?

Mrs Thumb No, Tom.
Not a bit!

Mr Thumb You must be the smallest boy in the world, Tom. If you don't grow, you'll be good-for-nothing.

Tom Please don't say that, father. Make me grow! PLEASE!

Mr Thumb We must give him more food, mother — good food.

Mrs Thumb But we DO give him good food.

Mr Thumb Let's try custard. Make him some custard, mother, with lots of milk.

Tom I don't like milk.

Mrs Thumb Milk is good for you, Tom.

Mr Thumb That's right! Make him some good, rich custard with lots of milk. I'm off to get the horse and cart ready for work. ★

Tom What are you putting in the custard, mother?

Mrs Thumb Milk! Milk is good for you.

Tom What else are you putting in?

Mrs Thumb A big egg.

Tom Good! I like eggs. Make the custard very sweet, mother. Put in lots of sugar. Now . . . can I try it?

Mrs Thumb No! Not yet.

Tom Let me try just a little bit.

Mrs Thumb No! Not yet. I have to go and get your little dish. ★

Tom Good!
She's gone!
I know what I'll do.
I'll get up here . . .
. . . and dip my finger in . . .
YUM!
  YUM!
    YUM!
This is good custard!
I'll get a bit more!

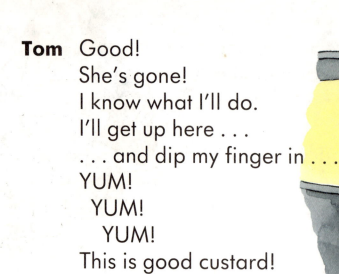

★
OW!
Mother!
Father!
HELP!

Mr Thumb ★ What's going on in here?
Mother! Where are you?
Tom! Where are you?

Tom HELP! HELP!

Mr Thumb Where's our Tom?

Mrs Thumb Tom! Where are you?

Tom IN THE CUSTARD!

Mrs Thumb Get him out!
Get him out!

Mr Thumb You little good-for-nothing! I said
EAT custard, not SWIM in it!

Tom It's all in my hair . . .
It's all in my ears . . .
It's all up my nose . . .

Mrs Thumb What CAN we do with him?

Mr Thumb   Put him to bed —
Without any bread!
That's what we can do with him.

Tom   BED — without any BREAD!
That won't make me grow.
I know! You can put
me to work.

Mr Thumb   WORK! What can a little
fellow like you do?

Mrs Thumb   You are too little to work, Tom.

Tom   No, I'm not!

Mrs Thumb   Yes, you are!

Tom   No, I'm not. I want to go to work.

Mr Thumb   If only you were bigger, you could
help me to drive the horse and cart.

Tom   I can! I can! Take me out to
the horse and cart. ★

Mr Thumb Well! Here we are! And here's the horse and cart . . . so show us what you can do.

Tom Put me up in the horse's ear!

Mr Thumb Whatever for?

Tom Put me up in the horse's ear and I'll show you.

Mrs Thumb No! No! You are too little to go up there, Tom.

Tom No, I'm not. You try me.

Mr Thumb Can you hear me, Tom?

Tom Yes!

Mr Thumb What's it like in there?

Tom Very nice! I like it!

Mrs Thumb I don't like it!
I don't like it at all!

Tom I do! And I'm the one who's inside.
GEE-UP, HORSE! GEE UP!

Mrs Thumb Look at that!

Tom STOP! WHOA, HORSE! WHOA!

Mr Thumb Well I never! Our little Tom
can drive the horse and cart.

Tom I told you I could do it.

Mr Thumb All right, Tom. We'll try you out. I'll go to the wood with my axe and you can bring the horse and cart along to me. ★

Mrs Thumb I don't like it, Tom. I don't like it at all.

Tom I do! I'm safe up here in the horse's ear! Watch me go, mother! ★ GEE-UP, HORSE! GEE-UP! ★ ★ Good-bye mother! Good-bye! ★ ★ ★

Tom in the Horse's Ear

In this part of the story you will read about:

Tom, who is on his way to the wood,

Snatch, who is a robber, and Grab, who is another robber.

Snatch and Grab are making plans to rob a big house.

Snatch Listen, Grab! When we get to the house we must creep round to the back.

Grab Is it a big house?

Snatch VERY big! Just think, Grab! The man who lives in that house has got bags and bags of gold. Soon we shall be rich!

Grab Ooo! GOLD! I want to be rich!

Snatch Look, Grab!
Can you see what
I see?

Grab What can you see, Snatch?

Snatch A horse and cart! It's coming our
way. We're in luck! We can get
a lift on that cart . . .
. . . GRAB!

Grab Yes, Snatch!

Snatch There's something funny about that horse
and cart. You have a look and tell me what
you can see.

Grab I can see a horse.

Snatch What else?

Grab I can see a cart.

Snatch But there's no one driving it!

Tom GEE-UP, HORSE! GEE-UP! ★ ★

Snatch Did you hear that, Grab?

Tom GEE-UP, HORSE! GEE-UP! ★ ★

Grab Snatch! There's no one there!

Snatch There's something funny going on here! We'll follow behind for a little way and see what happens.

Grab Not me!

Snatch Why not?

Grab I don't like it!

Snatch Never mind about not liking it! You come along with me and follow that cart! ★

Tom STOP! WHOA, HORSE! WHOA!

Grab Look at that!

Snatch It's stopped! There IS something VERY funny about this horse and cart.

Grab Come on, Snatch!
Let's go!

Snatch Not likely!

Tom Hallo there! Do you two want a ride on my cart?

Grab Not me!

Tom All right then! I'll drive on!

Snatch No! Don't do that. Just tell us where you are hiding.

Tom I'm up here in the horse's ear.

Snatch So that's where you are! What's your name, little man?

Tom Tom Thumb.

Snatch That's a good name for you. Come on, Grab! Up you get!

Grab I'm coming! ★
But I don't like it!

Snatch Come on, young fellow!
Come out of
that ear!
I want to have
a good look
at you.

Tom There's not much
to look at!
I'm very small.

Grab Come out!
We want to see you.

Tom All right! Here I am! Now what
do you think of me?

Snatch Well! Well! Well! I've never seen anything
like you before. Tell me, little man, how big
are you?

Tom I'm no bigger than my father's thumb!

Snatch Leave this to me, Grab!
Listen, Tom! Do you think that maybe
you're bigger than MY thumb?

Grab He is...

Snatch Shut up, Grab!
Leave this to me!
Listen Tom!
I've got an idea.
You come and stand
on my hand
and we'll see how
big you are.

Tom All right! Here I am!

Snatch Come on! Stand up tall!

Tom Well! What do you think of me?

Snatch I think you're the
smartest little fellow
I've ever seen...
... AND... ★
I'VE GOT YOU!

Grab Well done, Snatch!

Tom and the Robbers

In this part of the story you will read about:

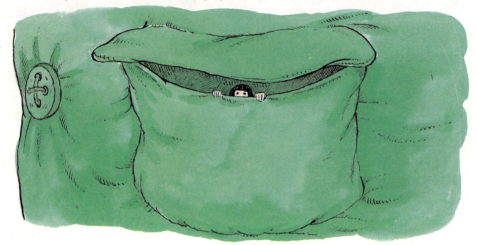

Tom, who is inside Snatch's pocket,

Snatch and Grab,

who are looking pleased because they have caught Tom.

Snatch and Grab are driving along the road on their way to the Big House. ★

Snatch Ho! Ho! Ho! I'm a clever one!

Grab Well done, Snatch!

Snatch Now for some of that gold.

Grab Ooo! We shall be rich, Snatch!

Snatch Can't you make this old horse go a bit faster, Grab?

Grab GEE-UP, HORSE! GEE-UP! ★

Snatch Give the old horse a slap, Grab.

Grab ★ GEE-UP, HORSE! GEE-UP! ★

Snatch Give him another one!

Grab ★ GEE-UP, HORSE! GEE-UP! ★ ★

Snatch That's better!

Tom HELP! HELP!

Grab Did you hear that, Snatch?

Snatch Ho! Ho! Ho! I heard, but I'm not listening! I bet our little fellow is having a bumpy ride down there in my pocket.

Tom LET ME OUT!
I can't get any air.
LET ME OUT!

Snatch Not likely! Ho! Ho! Ho! This little fellow is just what we need for our robbery.

Grab How can Tom help us?

Snatch Use your brains, Grab! This little Tom is so small he can get in anywhere.

Tom LET ME OUT!
LET ME OUT . . . OR I'LL DIE!

Grab Did you hear that, Snatch?

Snatch I heard . . . OUCH! Stop kicking, you little rascal, or I'll give YOU the next slap.

Tom Let me out . . . PLEASE!
Let me out and I'll do anything you say.

Grab Did you hear that, Snatch?

Tom I will! I will! Just let me out . . . PLEASE!

Grab Let him out, Snatch.

Snatch All right!
Out you come!

Tom Out at last!
Phew! It WAS hot in there.

Snatch So . . . You'll do anything we say, will you, Tom?

Tom Yes! I'll do anything.

Grab Will you rob the Big House for us?

Snatch Shut up, Grab!

Grab You said . . .

Snatch I said, 'SHUT UP!'

Tom What's he talking about, Snatch?

Snatch Nothing! Grab isn't doing the talking. I am.

Tom All right! What are YOU talking about, Snatch?

Snatch Well now, Tom. I've got a little plan.

Grab We are going to rob . . .

Snatch GRAB!

Grab Yes, Snatch?

Snatch What did I tell you to do?

Grab You told me to shut up.

Snatch SHUT UP, then!

Snatch Well now, Tom . . . Grab and I are on our way to a big house — a VERY BIG HOUSE . . . and it's full of bags . . . and the bags are full of . . . GOLD!

Tom Ooo! Can I go with you?

Snatch Well . . . we'll see!

Grab Snatch!

Snatch Yes?

Grab Can we give Tom a bit of the gold?

Snatch We'll see. Mmm! Maybe you've had a good idea, Grab. Maybe we could give Tom *one* little bit of the gold IF he does what we say.

Tom I'll do anything you say. If you give me a bit of gold I'll do anything.

Snatch Give the old horse a slap, Grab.

Grab GEE-UP, HORSE! GEE-UP! ★

Tom How shall we get into the house, Snatch?

Snatch Wait and see!

Grab I know . . .

Snatch Shut up, Grab! You drive the horse and leave everything else to me. ★ ★

Snatch Stop the horse, Grab.

Grab STOP, HORSE! STOP!

Tom WHOA, HORSE! WHOA! ★

Snatch Don't make so much noise! Now, listen to me. We'll tie the old horse up to this gatepost and creep round to the back of the house. ★ Come on! Follow me! ★

Grab I say, Snatch . . . ! ★

Snatch Ssh! Don't make so much noise.

Grab It's not me.
It's my boots!

Snatch Walk on your toes, then.

Tom Look at those windows.

Grab We can't get up there.

Tom Look at those big bars!

Grab We can't get in there!

Snatch WE can't . . . but this little Tom can!
Listen, Tom! We're going to put you
through those bars . . . and you're going
to hand the gold out to us.
Up you get! ★

Grab What can you see, Tom?

Tom BAGS!
Bags and bags of . . .

Snatch GOLD! Right! Get in! Open up the biggest bag and start handing the gold out through the bars.

Tom DO YOU WANT ALL OF IT?

Snatch Ssh! Don't make so much noise.

Tom HOW MUCH GOLD DO YOU WANT?

Grab Ssh! Ssh!

Tom DO YOU ROBBERS WANT ALL THIS GOLD?

Grab Shut him up, Snatch!
Shut him up!

Tom Aha! I know what I'll do! I'll make the sound of footsteps. ★
LISTEN ROBBERS! SOMEONE'S COMING!

Snatch Shut up, you fool!

Tom I know! I'll make the sound of a door opening. ★
LISTEN ROBBERS!
A DOOR'S OPENING!

Grab Come on, Snatch! Let's go!

Snatch But the gold! The gold! We haven't got . . .

Tom LISTEN ROBBERS! SOMEONE'S COMING!

Snatch Come on, Grab! I'm not stopping here! ★

Grab Nor me! ★

Tom Hurray! I'm free!
Now . . . how do I find my way home?

The Thumb Family Again

In this part of the story you will read about:

Mrs Thumb, who is all alone in the cottage,

Mr Thumb, who is on his way home from the wood,

and Tom, who is running away from the big house.

Mrs Thumb is coming into the kitchen.

Mr Thumb   I told you that our Tom is a good-for-nothing didn't I, mother?

Mrs Thumb   What has he done?

Mr Thumb   He hasn't DONE anything . . .

Mrs Thumb   But where is he?
Where's my Tom?

Mr Thumb   Isn't he here? He didn't come to the wood.

Mrs Thumb   But he went to the wood.
                He went with the horse and cart.

Mr Thumb   Well, he didn't come and I've walked all the way home...

Mrs Thumb   But where's my Tom?
                Where is he?
                Oh! Oh! Oh! ★

Mr Thumb   Don't cry, mother!

Mrs Thumb   ★ Tom! ★ Tom!

Mr Thumb   Don't worry! He'll turn up like a bad penny!

Mrs Thumb   You bad man!
                Take that! ★
                And that! ★
                And that! ★

Mr Thumb   Stop! Stop! Leave me alone, woman!

Mrs Thumb   You ... BAD MAN!
You ... GOOD-FOR-NOTHING!
TAKE THAT! ★

Mr Thumb   Leave me alone!
★ Listen! There's someone at the door ...

Tom   ★ MOTHER! FATHER! LET ME IN!

Mr Thumb   Did you hear that?

Tom   IT'S ME! TOM!

Mrs Thumb   Open the door. ★

Tom   Mother! Father! It's me! I'm home!

Mrs Thumb   Oh Tom! Tom! You've come home!

Mr Thumb You young rascal!
You good-for-nothing!
Where have you been? ★

Tom Stop that, father!
Leave me alone!

Mrs Thumb Yes, leave him alone.
Leave him alone or I'll . . .

Mr Thumb All right! All right! But where have you been and where's my horse and cart?

Tom It's at the Big House where the robbers took me to do a robbery.

Mr Thumb Now then, Tom Thumb! Don't try telling us one of your tales . . .

Tom It's true! It's true!

Mrs Thumb Go on, Tom!
Tell us!

Tom Well . . . these robbers had a plan to rob the Big House . . .

Mr Thumb What were their names?

Tom Snatch and Grab.

Mr Thumb Snatch and Grab! It IS one of your tales, Tom. You're making it up.

Mrs Thumb Are you making it up, Tom?

Tom No, I'm not.

Mrs Thumb Go on, then.

Tom Snatch and Grab put me through the window bars to get the . . . GOLD!

Mr Thumb He IS making it up!

Tom What's this, then?

Mrs Thumb Look at that!

Mr Thumb It IS a gold coin.
A real gold coin!

Tom Do you believe
me now, father?

Mr Thumb Yes! I believe you, Tom. You've got a gold coin. We're rich!

Tom Am I a good-for-nothing now, father?

Mr Thumb Ho! Ho! Ho! You're good-for-something now, my boy. What shall we give him, mother?

Tom Give me some food!

Mrs Thumb What do you want, Tom?

Tom Custard! Lots and lots of custard!

Out to Lunch

with Brian Turner

ANGLIA TELEVISION

Water, water everywhere ... but Turner kept smiling, despite the encroaching tide at Brightlingsea (left) and threatening thunder in Cambridge (right).

introduction

There's an old saying: "If you can't stand the heat, get out of the kitchen." So we did!

At the time, *al fresco* cooking seemed such a good idea. What better way, I thought, to show off the region's finest produce than to present it in its natural setting. As long as the sun shone we would be fine!

But I'd forgotten we were working with 'a professional.' Professional chefs are different to you and me. They like it hot – and I mean hot! The kind of heat that singes your eyebrows the moment you open the oven door ... the sort that gives you a suntan the instant you get anywhere near the stove.

When Brian Turner first saw our trestle table he laughed – nervously! When we produced the single ring portable gas burner he went pale. And by the time we had carted table, stove and ingredients three-quarters of a mile across the salt marshes he was checking his contract to see if he could find a possible way out!

Of course, being a true professional he not only coped – but shone. Just like the sun.

But there were days when the sun didn't shine ... and we found ourselves cooking beside the river Cam with thunder and lightning just around the corner! Or we had to stop halfway through a recipe at a fruit farm and gather round under umbrellas to prevent the pastry going soggy!

Turner kept smiling – even when we had to call in a beach shop to buy a windbreak because a gale blew out the gas burners!

Of course, it's not just the chef who has to adapt to the demands of *al fresco* cooking. Spare a thought too for Annie, our wonderful home economist – somewhere just out of camera shot, sitting on the ground, chopping carrots, peeling potatoes, making stock. And for her car, loaded down with over-ripe tomatoes, and two day old Crab Gratin ....

Still, by the end of the series Turner, Annie, the trestle table and the portable stove had become firm friends. Who am I kidding? The day finally came when we gave Brian the chance to cook in a proper restaurant kitchen. Within seconds the crew were reaching for handkerchiefs to wipe away the sweat. Turner, meanwhile, was as cool as a cucumber – here was a chef who had finally come home!

PAUL FREEMAN
Series Producer

*Roast Goose and all the trimmings
– see page 28 for Brian Turner's Christmas special.*

contents

North Norfolk 1
Samphire and Asparagus Salad 7
Mullet with Mushroom Sauce 8
Spicy Crab Gratin 9

Peterborough 2
Timpana 10
Sausage and Mash 11
Bracciola 12
Frosted Carrot Cake 13

Cambridge 3
Chicken and Leek Jalousie 14
Classic Leg of Lamb 15
Summer Berry Fool 16

Essex 4
Poached Oysters in Champagne Butter Sauce 17
Pork with Pancetta and Caramelised Apples 18
Chocolate Truffle Terrine 19

Suffolk 5
Baked Cod with a Basil and Parsley Topping 20
Honey Glazed Bacon Pot Roast 21
Frittata 22

Breckland/West Norfolk 6
Barbecued Trout with Spinach and Bacon 23
Lavender Honey Ice Cream 24
Honey and Pistachio Sponge Pudding 25
Spinach, Cheese & Artichoke Puddings 26
Crispy Turkey Escalopes 27

Christmas Special 7
Roast Goose with Apple & Chestnut Stuffing 28
Prune and Apple Stuffing 28
Mulled Wine 29
Braised Red Cabbage 29
Egg Nog 30
Chocolate, Rum & Chestnut Roulade 31
Roast Beef & Yorkshire Pudding 32
Honey & Chilli Roast Parsnips 33
Canapés 34

Northamptonshire 8
Pumpkin Risotto 35
Roast Pheasant with Apples & Calvados 36
Petti di Pollo alla Yolanda 37
Mushrooms on the Wild Side 38

Newmarket/Ely 9
Braised Celery au Gratin 40
Celery and Apple Soup 41
An 'Offaly' Good Breakfast! 42
Chicken en Cocotte 43

Woburn/Olney 10
Pan-Fried Venison Steaks 44
Salmon Niçoise 45
Crêpes Suzette 46

Useful Addresses *47*

Measurements *inside back cover*

programme 1 — # Samphire and Asparagus Salad

Ingredients:

- 8 oz (225g) samphire [see note]
- 16 spears of asparagus – trimmed and peeled if woody
- 4 fl oz (120ml) good quality olive oil
- 1 fl oz (25ml) white wine vinegar
- 2 level tsp French mustard
- 4 tomatoes, skinned, seeded and diced
- 1 bunch chives
- handful of chervil if available or use flat leaf parsley

Method:

Wash the samphire in plenty of cold water. Drain well.

Bring a large pan of water to the boil. Add the samphire and boil until tender. Drain well and refresh in plenty of cold water to retain some colour. NB Do not add salt – samphire is very salty.

Place asparagus on a chopping board. Using a potato peeler remove the peel from the stem.

Cook the asparagus for 2-3 minutes in boiling salted water.

Place the olive oil in a basin. Whisk in the white wine vinegar, followed by the mustard. Whisk until smooth. Season.

Remove the skin from the tomatoes by dropping into boiling water briefly. Cool quickly and the skin should peel away easily. Cut into four. Remove the seeds and dice evenly.

Chop the chervil if using or flat leaved parsley and the chives.

Add the tomato concassé to the dressing, followed by the chopped herbs.

Place the asparagus and samphire in a bowl. Pour the dressing over. Toss well.

Arrange on individual plates.

Serve with seafood and hunks of French bread.

Samphire

Not strictly a seaweed, samphire grows in marshy shallows, salty mudflats and along the shoreline in bright green tufts approximately 10" high. It makes a delicious salad; or serve as a starter with a fishy meal – just boil until tender, dip in melted butter and eat with fingers. Do not salt the cooking water – samphire has lots of natural salt.

Mullet with Mushroom Sauce

programme 1

Ingredients:

2 lb (900g) grey mullet fillets
¼ pint (150ml) dry white wine
¼ pint (150ml) fish stock
2 bay leaves
3-4 sprigs fresh thyme
handful chopped parsley
4 oz (125g) unsalted butter OR 2 tbsp olive oil
12 oz (350g) baby button mushrooms sliced finely
2 hard boiled eggs, finely chopped
4 oz (100g) fine brown breadcrumbs

Method:

Melt half the butter and oil in a large deep frying pan. Add the mushrooms. Cook for about five minutes.

Add the wine and fish stock to the pan, followed by the bay leaves and thyme sprigs. Bring to the boil. Season. Reduce to a simmer.

Add the prepared mullet fillets to the stock. Cover the pan and cook until you see a milky fluid between the scales. Do not overcook. Remove the mullet fillets. Keep warm.

Increase the heat, bring the stock back to the boil and cook until the stock is reduced by at least half.

Add small cubes of butter to the sauce, followed by the double cream. Whisk well.

Stir in the chopped parsley and hard-boiled egg. Place the mullet fillets on individual plates.

Spoon the sauce over. Garnish with a little reserved chopped hard-boiled egg and parsley.

The fruits of the sea – Brian nabs a crab at Cromer.

programme 1 — *Spicy Crab Gratin*

serves 4

Ingredients:

2 boiled crabs, approximately 1¼ lb (550g) each
¼ pint (150ml) fish stock or use a cube
2 oz (50g) unsalted butter
2 medium red peppers, cored and seeded and diced finely
2 cloves garlic
½ level tsp cayenne pepper
2 tsp Tabasco, red or green
4 oz (100g) fine breadcrumbs
seasoning

Method:

Remove the meat from the crabs. Mix the white and brown meat together.

Melt the unsalted butter in a frying pan. Add the garlic and cook for 2-3 minutes.

Add the finely diced red pepper and cook for a few minutes until the pepper begins to soften.

Stir in the cayenne pepper and Tabasco. Mix well and heat through.

Gently stir the stock into the spicy mixture. Bring to the boil, reduce the heat and simmer until the sauce is reduced slightly.

Fold in the crab meat. Heat through.

Place the crab mixture back in the washed crab shells or in a shallow gratin dish.

Sprinkle the spicy mixture with the seasoned breadcrumbs.

Dot with butter and place under the grill for a few minutes until golden brown.

Serve with crisp green salad and crusty bread, and a glass of chilled white wine.

Crabs

If you are boiling your own crab it should be done in plenty of boiling salted water approximately 5 oz (150g) salt to 8 pints (4.5 litres) water. However, the most popular and easiest way is to purchase a boiled crab – but preferably undressed. This way the 'meat' is much fresher and more moist.

programme 2 — Timpana

Ingredients:

½ onion, finely chopped
1 tbsp olive oil
2 tomatoes, skinned, seeded and diced
½ pint (75ml) vegetable stock
4 oz (100g) chicken livers
4 oz (100g) chopped bacon
3 oz (75g) Ricotta cheese
2 hard boiled eggs
8 oz (225g) puff pastry
4 oz (100g) minced beef
4 oz (100g) minced pork
8 oz (225g) macaroni
2 eggs
2 tbsp single cream
2 oz (50g) grated Parmesan
freshly ground black pepper

Method:

Sauté the onion in the olive oil, add the stock and the skinned, de-seeded tomatoes.

Bring to the boil and simmer for 5 minutes.

Clean and dice the chicken livers. Add to the pan.

Add the chopped bacon followed by the minced beef and minced pork.

Cook the macaroni in plenty of boiling salted water until it is *al dente*. Refresh. Add the macaroni to the meat mixture.

In a basin beat together the eggs and cream. Fold in the grated cheese and chopped hard boiled eggs.

Add the minced meat sauce to the egg mixture.

Roll out the puff pastry and line a greased ovenproof pie dish.

Pile the pasta and meat mixture into the pastry case and top with the remainder of the rolled out pastry.

Brush generously with beaten egg.

Bake at 190°C/375°F/gas mark 5 for 35-40 minutes until pastry is well risen and golden brown.

 *programme 2* — Simply the Best *Sausage and Mash*

RECIPE A
Ingredients:

2 lb (900g) potatoes, peeled and cut into quarters
1 bunch spring onions, finely chopped (use the green parts too)
2 fat cloves of garlic
4 tbsp olive oil
1 lb (450g) good quality sausages
onion gravy

Method:

Place the potatoes in a large pan, cover with cold water and bring to the boil. Simmer for 15-20 minutes until tender.

Drain the potatoes through a sieve.

Return to the pan, season well, add the olive oil and mix well.

Meanwhile sauté the garlic and spring onion together. Place the onion mixture into the potatoes, mix well and check the seasoning.

Pile the mashed potatoes onto a large platter with the sausages on top.

Serve with good thick onion gravy.

RECIPE B
Ingredients:

2 lb (900g) potatoes, peeled and cut into quarters
4 oz (100g) unsalted butter, softened
¼ pint (150ml) double cream OR whipping cream
1 lb (450g) good quality sausages
onion gravy

Method:

Prepare and cook the potatoes as in method A. After draining return to the pan as before.

Add the softened butter, plenty of salt and pepper, and mix well.

Gradually beat the cream into the potatoes.

Pile into a dish and top with the grilled sausages and onion gravy.

Choosing Potatoes for Mashing

Potatoes are roughly divided into groups suited to specific methods of cooking. Some are floury, some mealy, some creamy and waxy etc. A number of potato varieties are good all-rounders, however.
Try these for a good 'mash':

King Edwards: *Large main crop potato. Cream coloured floury flesh. Excellent all-rounder. Also good for roasting.*

Pentland Squire: *Main crop potato, white skinned and white fleshed. Floury texture. Good cooking qualities.*

Cara: *Creamy flesh, pink-fringed skin. Good all-rounder.*

Carlingford: *White skinned and white flesh*

Maris Piper: *Thin white skin and cream coloured flesh. Good flavour. Excellent for boiling and mashing.*

Romano: *Red skin with cream flesh. Good all-rounder.*

programme **2** — *Bracciola* guest recipe by Lucia Di'Ioria

Ingredients:

- 4 pieces frying steak
- 1 chopped onion
- chopped parsley
- 2 chopped garlic cloves
- salt and pepper
- Parmesan cheese
- cocktail sticks
- olive oil
- 1 large jar tomato sauce (eg Passato)
- 1 large tin tomato puree
- pasta

Method:

Hammer steak until nice and thin and cut into 2"-3" by 4"-5" pieces. Sprinkle with some onion, chopped parsley, chopped garlic, salt and pepper, and Parmesan cheese.

Roll up each steak piece and secure with a cocktail stick through the middle.

Place in a saucepan with some olive oil, and more chopped onion, and brown. Add the jar of tomato sauce (such as Passato), the tomato puree, salt and pepper and some more garlic.

Rinse out the puree tin with water, add, and simmer the mixture for 1¾-2 hours.

Cook the pasta, mix in the sauce and sprinkle with Parmesan to serve with the meat rolls. Accompany with a mixed salad of lettuce, cucumber, tomato, olive oil, vinegar and salt.

Supping a pint at Peterborough's beer festival

programme 2 — Frosted Carrot Cake

For the cake:
Ingredients:

10 oz (275g) self raising flour	
1 level tsp baking powder	
8 oz (225g) margarine or butter	
8 oz (225g) unrefined soft brown sugar	
4 medium eggs	
4 oz (100g) sultanas	
1 lb (450g) grated carrots	
2 level tbsp ground coriander	
4 oz (100g) very finely chopped apricots	

Method:

Sieve the teaspoon of baking powder together with the self raising flour.

Cream the margarine/butter and sugar together until soft and creamy and lighter in colour.

Add the beaten egg a little at a time and whisk into the mixture.

Fold in the flour and baking powder, along with the ground coriander.

Add the grated carrot, finely chopped apricots and sultanas. Mix together well.

Spoon into a 8" double lined and greased loose bottomed cake tin. Level the surface.

Bake at 180°C/350°F for 1-1¼ hours or until a skewer inserted in the centre comes out clean.

NB If the cake is over browning place a piece of parchment loosely over the top.

for the frosting:
Ingredients:

- 8 oz (225g) full fat cream cheese
- 2oz (50g) butter
- 4 oz (100g) sieved icing sugar
- a few walnut halves for decoration
- 1 tsp vanilla essence

Method:

Place the butter in a basin. Cream until smooth with the soft cheese.

Gradually add the sieved icing sugar. Mix in the vanilla essence.

Spoon the frosting over the cooled cake and make a rough pattern with a fork or palette knife.

NB The cake needs to be refrigerated once you have put the topping on. The cake will keep well in a tin without the frosting.

programme 3 — Chicken and Leek Jalousie

Ingredients:

1 lb (450g) puff pastry
8 oz (225g) cooked chicken, diced
8 oz (225g) leeks, finely sliced
2 tbsp grain mustard
pinch of five spice powder
¼ pint (150ml) créme frâiche
1 egg, beaten
2 tbsp sesame seeds
2 oz (50g) butter, unsalted

Method:

Divide the pastry into two portions. Roll out the puff pastry into a rectangle 11½" x 8" (30 x 20mm).

Dice the chicken and place in a large bowl.

Melt the butter in a pan and add the finely shredded leeks. Cook until softened. Season.

Add the grainy mustard and five spice powder. Stir in the créme frâiche.

Pour the leek mix into the bowl and mix with the chicken.

Brush the edges of the pastry with beaten egg. Spoon the filling down the centre of the pastry rectangle. Roll out the second reserved piece of pastry. Place over the filling. Seal the edges well.

Make several cuts in the pastry. Brush with beaten egg. Sprinkle with 2 tablespoons of sesame seeds.

Bake for 30-35 minutes until the pastry is well risen and golden brown.

Serve with a salad of apple and potato.

Delicious eaten hot or cold.

programme 3 — *Classic Leg of Lamb*

Ingredients:

1 leg lamb joint approx 4 lb (1,800kg) in weight (see note below)
8 oz (225g) mushrooms, finely diced
4 oz (125g) pork sausage meat
2 tbsp finely chopped parsley
2 oz (50g) fine fresh breadcrumbs
1 egg, beaten
3 cloves of garlic
3-4 sprigs of rosemary
1 lb (450g) large carrots
1 lb (450g) potatoes
1 dozen baby onions

NB Ask your butcher to remove the bone from the lamb to make a pocket for the stuffing.

Method:

Mince the mushrooms and sweat off in a pan for about 5 minutes. Drain off the moisture.

Add the sausagemeat, breadcrumbs, parsley, eggs and plenty of seasoning. Mix well.

Stuff the lamb, but do not overfill otherwise the mixture will expand and overflow. Cook any spare filling separately.

Tie up the lamb and place a piece of foil on the end of the meat to secure the stuffing.

Press some slices of garlic into the lamb and also sprigs of rosemary if available.

Heat 3-4 tbsp oil in a roasting tin. Seal off the leg of lamb briefly then place in a hot oven for about 20 minutes per pound.

Using a melon baller cut out shapes from the carrot and potato.

Heat a little butter in a pan and add a little caster sugar. Cook the carrots until caramelised.

In two separate pans cook the potatoes and baby onions – they need to be golden brown.

Carve the lamb into thick slices onto a platter and pile the vegetables alongside.

Serve with mint sauce and good gravy.

programme 3 — *Summer Berry Fool*

Ingredients:

1 lb (450g) mixed summer berries: loganberries, raspberries, strawberries etc

¼ pint (150ml) double cream, whipped until 'floppy'

¼ pint (150ml) Greek yoghurt

squeeze of lemon juice

for the fruit coulis:

1 lb (450g) raspberries pureed with

1 tbsp icing sugar (sieve if necessary)

ground black pepper

Method:

Place the berries in a bowl and mash roughly with a fork. Sweeten, if required, to taste.

Lightly whip the double cream and fold in the Greek yoghurt.

Fold the berry puree lightly into the fruit and chill.

Pile the 'fool' into a pastry case and top with a scattering of whole berries.

Drizzle with the fruit coulis and dredge lightly with icing sugar.

Variation:

Sprinkle whole berries with a generous amount of black pepper.

Add ½ pint fruit coulis and marinate for ½ hour.

Layer up the marinated puree with the peppered berries in a tall sundae glass.

Decorate with mint leaves, serve well chilled.

programme 4

Poached Oysters in Champagne Butter Sauce

Ingredients:

1 dozen oysters, shucked – see notes

4 oz (100g) finely chopped shallots

¼ pint (150ml) Champagne

2 oz (50g) unsalted butter

8 oz (225g) baby spinach; leaves and stems removed

¼ pint (150ml) double cream

Method:

Prepare the spinach – remove any stalks, and rinse.

Place in a pan with a little butter and cook only briefly until the spinach 'wilts'.

Place spinach in oyster shells.

Place Champagne in a pan, bring to the boil, then reduce heat and poach oysters briefly for about one minute.

Remove oysters and put back in shells on top of the spinach.

Increase the heat and reduce the poaching liquor down until you have about one tablespoon left.

Season. Gradually whisk in the double cream and the butter.

Spoon the hot sauce over the oysters and spinach.

Oysters

The outside shell of the oyster is tough and flinty. The concentric whorls show how the shell has grown and changed in shape and size. There is a flat top shell and a lipped lower shell with a hinge at the narrow end.

Unopened oysters, which are tightly shut, will keep for a few days in a cold place. Do not open the oysters until you need them. To split an oyster – known as SHUCKING – you will need a special oyster knife with a broad wooden handle. (Please don't be tempted to open oysters with a kitchen knife – it is very dangerous).

Shucking the oyster

Grip the oyster firmly in a cloth and carefully insert an oyster knife into the hinged edge. Twist to prise open the shell.

*Still holding the shell firmly slide the blade along the inside of the upper shell to sever the first of the two muscles. Lift off the upper shell without spillage of any juices. Slide the blade **under** the oyster to sever the second muscle beneath it.*

17

Pork with Pancetta and Caramelised Apples

serves 4

Ingredients:

2 fillets of pork, trimmed and with fat removed
6 oz (150g) breadcrumbs
1 large onion, finely chopped
1 egg, beaten
a good handful of chopped sage leaves
6 oz (175g) pancetta (Italian streaky bacon: can be bought smoked or plain) or streaky bacon or smoked middle bacon
½ pint (300ml) apple juice (or use half stock/half juice)
¼ pint (150ml) double cream
4 red skinned apples, cored but not peeled
2-3 tbsp olive oil

Method:

Slit the pork open lengthwise and open out.

Place the breadcrumbs, onion and chopped sage in a mixing bowl. Add enough beaten egg to moisten. Season well.

Divide the mixture between the two fillets. Press in well.

Wrap the pancetta slices around the fillets. Tie with string for extra safety if necessary.

Heat the oil. Seal off the fillets, then add the apple juice. Cover and cook for approximately 40-45 minutes.

Remove the pork. Keep warm.

Bring the apple juice to the boil and reduce until you have 3-4 tablespoons of thick juice left.

Gradually add the double cream and whisk in about one tablespoon of butter. Season.

Meanwhile, in a separate pan, melt the rest of the butter with the sugar and fry the apple slices until caramelised and golden brown.

Serve the pork, dressed with the sauce and garnished with the caramelised apples. Accompany with seasonal vegetables.

Chocolate Truffle Terrine

Ingredients:

for the mousse mixture:

- 1 lb (450g) good quality dessert chocolate
- 5 tbsp rum or Amaretto
- 4 tbsp golden syrup
- 1 pint (600ml) double cream
- ¼ pint (150ml) whipping cream

for the sponge:

- 3 oz (75g) plain flour
- 3 oz (75g) caster sugar
- 3 eggs, medium size
- 1 oz (25g) cocoa, sifted

Method:

First make the sponge.

Place the eggs and sugar in a large mixing bowl. Whisk with an electric beater until the mixture changes colour and is thick enough to leave a trail when you lift the whisk out of the mixture.

Fold in the sifted flour. Divide the mixture into two equal quantities.

Sieve the cocoa into one of the mixtures and fold in evenly. Place both chocolate and plain mixtures into two large piping bags.

Pipe alternate diagonal lines of mixture into a greased and lined Swiss roll tin. Bake at 190°C/375°F/gas mark 5 for 25-30 minutes until 'springy' to the touch. Cool on a wire rack.

Split cake into three equal portions and trim to fit a loaf tin which has been lined with cling film.

Place one striped chocolate layer of cake in the base of the loaf tin. Drizzle with a little rum.

Meanwhile make the chocolate mousse mixture.

Place the broken up chocolate in a clean bowl and melt carefully.

Stir in the rum and golden syrup. Mix well.

Whip the cream until it is floppy. Carefully fold the cream into the chocolate mix.

Pour a layer of chocolate mix into the loaf tin then top with a layer of sponge.

Repeat the process, ending with a layer of sponge.

Bring the cling film over the torte and freeze overnight. Leave in the 'fridge for 1-2 hours before serving.

Decorate with scrolls of whipping cream and redcurrants or seasonal berries. Dust with icing sugar.

programme 5 — Baked Cod with Basil & Parsley Topping

Ingredients:

4 pieces of cod – approx 5oz (125g) each
8 oz (225g) sugar snap peas
8 oz (225g) new potatoes, cooked and halved
8 oz (225g) tomatoes, deseeded and quartered
6 oz (175g) fresh breadcrumbs
a good handful of fresh basil leaves, shredded
a good handful of freshly chopped parsley
2 fl oz (50ml) olive oil
2 oz (50g) unsalted butter
2 tbsp horseradish mustard
1 egg, beaten

Method:

Skin the cod and remove any bones with a pair of tweezers.

Season the cod and brush generously with horseradish mustard

Shred the basil, finely chop the parsley and place in a mixing bowl. Add breadcrumbs, seasoning and beaten egg. Season well.

Pile the topping on the fish, pressing it to help it stick.

Melt the butter and olive oil in a large frying pan. Toss the halved potatoes and sugar snap peas in the pan and season. Do not brown.

Grease a shallow baking dish or small roasting tin. Place the tomato quarters, potatoes and sugar snap peas in the dish.

Place the herbed cod on the vegetables; drizzle with olive oil.

Roast at 190°C/375°F/gas mark 5 for approximately 15-20 minutes, until the fish flakes easily.

Honey Glazed Bacon Pot Roast

programme 5 — Honey Glazed Bacon Pot Roast

Ingredients:

(serves 6-8)

3 lb (1.3kg) collar bacon

1 onion, stuck with 6-8 cloves

1-2 bay leaves

¼ pint (125ml) water

¼ pint (125ml) dry cider or apple juice

6-8 peppercorns

2 large carrots, cut into strips (julienne)

1 onion, sliced

1 lb (450g) swede, peeled and diced

4 celery stalks, chopped

2 oz (50g) butter, unsalted

One of the best cuts of bacon for this recipe is **collar bacon**. *It is further divided into two cuts:* **prime collar** *– which weighs about 6 lb (2.7kg) and is the best joint for boiling, either whole for a celebration or large party, or cut into smaller manageable pieces; and* **end collar**: *about 2 lb (1kg) in weight - an excellent economical cut great for boiling or baking, but do soak first.*

for the glaze:

1 tbsp made mustard

2 tbsp unrefined muscovado sugar

1-2 tbsp runny honey

Method:

Place the bacon collar in a pan with the onion, bay leaf and peppercorns.

Pour in the water and cider and top up with a little extra liquid so that the bacon is just covered.

Place lid on pan, bring to the boil and simmer for 40 minutes.

Melt the butter in a separate pan and toss in all the prepared vegetables. Turn them frequently for 10-15 minutes. Season with plenty of pepper.

Place the warm vegetables in the base of a casserole dish or roasting tin.

Drain the liquid from the bacon, reserving the liquid, and place the bacon joint on the bed of vegetables. Spoon over about 4 tablespoons of the reserved liquid. Add the onion with cloves.

Cover with a lid and bake for about 1¼ hours at 180°C/350°F/gas mark 4. Test with a skewer – the bacon should feel very tender.

Remove from the oven, carefully strip off the rind and about ¼" layer of fat. Score the remaining fat on the bacon into diamond shapes.

Mix together the honey, mustard and brown sugar to a fairly stiff paste. Spread over the top of the bacon.

Place under a very hot grill to caramelise the sugar and give a good glaze.

Serve the bacon joint on a bed of vegetables. Garnish with bay leaves and accompany with a fruity chutney.

Glaze: mix the sugar and mustard together. Add enough honey to make a stiffish paste.

programme 5 — *Frittata*

Ingredients:

5-6 large eggs
1 red pepper, finely diced
1 yellow pepper, finely diced
8 oz (225g) waxy new potatoes (eg charlottes), diced
2 oz (50g) unsalted butter
seasoning
½ medium onion, finely chopped

Method:

Prepare all the vegetables and melt the butter in a large frying pan.

Add the onion and soften for about 5 minutes.

Add the potatoes and cook, stirring frequently until they are softened but not brown.

Add the peppers, stir well and season generously.

Beat the eggs, turn up the heat slightly and pour into the pan. Push the edges of the frittata towards the centre, letting the runny egg flood to the edges. This will then set.

Turn down the heat and let the frittata cook for about 5-8 minutes until just set.

Meanwhile pre-heat the grill and place the frying pan under the grill for about 3-4 minutes until the surface is golden brown.

Serve hot or cold cut into wedges with a tossed mixed salad and hunks of French bread.

Barbecued Trout with Spinach and Bacon

Ingredients:

4 trout, gutted and cleaned

8 oz (225g) baby spinach

8 rashers smoked streaky bacon

4 oz (100g) bacon lardons

1 large onion, diced

¼ pint (125ml) red wine

2 oz (50g) unsalted butter

4 oz (100g) mushrooms, sliced

Method:

Melt the butter in a roomy pan, add the onion and soften.

Place the roughly chopped washed spinach into the pan with the onion and cook briefly – until the spinach wilts. Remove and cool briefly.

Season the spinach and onion stuffing mixture with salt and plenty of pepper. Use to fill the four trout.

Wrap two rashers of bacon around each trout and secure with a cocktail stick.

Place the trout on the barbecue and cook for 8-10 minutes until crispy on the outside and succulent in the middle.

Meanwhile make the sauce.

Cook the bacon lardons for 5-6 minutes then add the sliced mushrooms and continue to stir. Season.

Pour in the red wine, bring to the boil then reduce the heat and simmer for 5 minutes.

Stir in about ½ oz (15g) butter to give the sauce extra gloss.

Remove the trout from the barbecue and place on a warmed platter. Pour the sauce over.

Serve with a green salad and granary bread or buttered new potatoes.

programme 6 — *Lavender Honey Ice Cream*

guest recipe by Fiona Dickson, honey supplier

Ingredients:

10-15 flower heads of lavender
½ cup water
2 packets of 8 fl oz (250ml) soya cream
8 oz (225g) liquid heather or dark honey
pollen granules and extra flower heads to garnish

Pollen granules available from most good health food shops or local beekeeper.

Method:

Bring water and lavender heads to boil and steep for 10 minutes. Cool and strain, reserving lavender-scented liquor. Pour soya cream and honey into mixing bowl, add lavender liquor and mix well.

Pour into ice-cream maker and freeze-mix for approximately 20 minutes until ice-cream consistency is reached. (If no ice-cream maker is available semi-freeze mixture in freezer for approximately two hours or until half frozen, and whizz in food processor until creamy. Quickly re-freeze in suitable container).

Decorate scoops of ice cream with sprinkled pollen granules and lavender heads.

Honey

'Dew distilled from the stars and the rainbow' *was how Aristotle described honey. We may be less poetic today but just as enthusiastic about its taste and nutritional value.*

Honey consists of glucose (35%), fructose (40%) and water (18%). Used mainly as a sweetener, it also has a medicinal value, in wound dressings and for sore throats. In the Middle Ages, monks made honey into mead, and used the wax for candles and document seals.

There are two types of honey commonly available in supermarkets – liquid, and set. Set honey can be rendered runny by placing the jar in hot water.

Or you can buy honey from local beekeepers. There are around 40,000 beekeepers in the UK, and many sell their produce from the garden gate.

 # Honey and Pistachio Sponge Pudding

Ingredients:

9 oz (250g) unrefined soft brown sugar

9 oz (250g) softened butter

5 eggs, size 3 or medium

2 level tbsp runny honey

6 oz (150g) chopped pistachio nuts

3 tbsp double cream

14 oz (400g) self raising flour

Topping:

2 level tbsp honey, warmed

2 oz (50g) chopped pistachios

to serve: clotted cream

Method:

Cream the butter and sugar together until light and fluffy.

Add the beaten eggs gradually. Mix well.

Fold in the sieved flour.

Add the chopped pistachios and double cream. Mix well.

Either grease a large 2 pint pudding basin well, or use individual moulds – again well greased.

Place a little warmed honey in the base of the moulds, followed by the pistachios.

Spoon the pudding mix over – fill the moulds two-thirds full. Cover with a ring of greaseproof paper.

Place in a steamer. The large pudding will take 1½-2 hours, the individual puddings about 25 minutes. They are cooked when well risen and golden brown.

Turn out the puddings. Serve with clotted cream and a sprig of mint.

NB the puddings are delicious eaten hot or cold.

Spinach, Goat Cheese & Artichoke Puddings

guest recipe by Vanessa Scott of Strattons Hotel, Swaffham, Norfolk

Filling ingredients:

2 oz (50g) butter
1 onion, peeled and chopped
3 individual English goat cheeses (eg Crottin produced by Gedi in Hertfordshire)
8-10 oz (225-275g) Jerusalem artichokes, scrubbed, trimmed and sliced
2 lb (900g) washed and dried spinach
salt and freshly ground pepper

Pastry ingredients:

10 oz (275g) self-raising flour
1½ tsp pesto
5 oz (150g) shredded vegetable suet
¼ pint (150ml) cold water to bind

Sauce ingredients:

1 small onion
1 tbsp olive oil
1 lb ripe tomatoes, roughly chopped
8 oz (225g) Jerusalem artichokes, scrubbed, trimmed and sliced
1½ pints (900ml) vegetable stock
salt and freshly ground white pepper
handful of chopped fresh basil leaves

Method:

Sweat the onion and sliced Jerusalem artichokes in the butter with the salt and black pepper. Add a small amount of vegetable stock and continue to sweat until the artichokes are just cooked, and coated in a thick sticky sauce.

Steam the spinach for a couple of minutes then drain well.

Slice the goat cheeses into thin slivers.

Stir the well-drained spinach into the warm artichoke mixture, add the goat cheese, and mix well. The goat cheese will melt with the warmth of the mixture.

To make the pastry sift the flour and a pinch of salt into a bowl. Add the suet and approximately ¼ pint of water and the pesto; mix to a firm dough.

Reserve a quarter for the lids, and roll out the remainder to line the base and sides of six small pudding basins. Spoon the filling into the centre of the lined moulds. Dampen the pastry around the top of the basins with water. Roll out reserved pastry to form lids. Cover with buttered greaseproof and foil lids. Steam for 25 minutes. Leave to stand for three minutes then invert onto six dinner plates.

Sauce:

Sweat the onion until translucent in the olive oil.

Add the tomatoes including any juice, the artichokes and half the stock. Simmer gently until the artichokes and onion are soft.

Allow to cool slightly, then make a puree in a blender and sieve into a clean saucepan.

Stir in the remaining stock, bring to the boil and simmer for 8-10 minutes. Season to taste and add chopped fresh basil.

Serve in a pool around the goat cheese puddings, with crunchy roast new potatoes and garlic.

Crispy Turkey Escalopes

serves 4

Ingredients:

- 4 turkey breast steaks
- 4 thick slices ham, fat removed
- 4 oz (100g) Gruyère cheese, cut into strips
- 2 cloves of garlic
- 2 oz (50g) butter, unsalted
- handful of freshly chopped parsley
- 4 oz (100g) fresh white or brown breadcrumbs
- 2 eggs, beaten

Method:

Beat out the turkey steaks between sheets of cling film.

Place a slice of ham over the turkey, followed by matchstick pieces of Gruyère cheese.

Fold the turkey around the cheese and ham to make a parcel. Seal and secure with a cocktail stick if necessary.

Dip the escalope in the beaten egg then toss in the breadcrumbs – this can be done twice for a better seal.

Melt the butter in a frying pan. Add the garlic and soften, then add the parsley.

Place the escalope in the pan and cook on each side for about 8-10 minutes, but check to ensure it is fully cooked. The escalopes are ready when they are golden brown and crisp.

Serve with a julienne of carrot and courgette and new potatoes.

Roast Goose with Apple and Chestnut Stuffing

Ingredients:

12 lb (5.4kg) goose

for the stuffing:

1 lb (450g) Bramley apples, diced

1 lb (450g) peeled chestnuts, diced

1 large onion, finely chopped

8 oz (225g) sausagemeat

2 medium eggs, beaten

1 tbsp chopped thyme

seasoning

4 oz (100g) breadcrumbs

Method:

Sweat the onion in butter, add the apples and sauté for 3-4 minutes. Remove from the pan and cool.

Break up the sausagemeat and mix in the breadcrumbs and diced chestnuts. Fold in the cooked apple, herbs and onion.

Season and bind with enough beaten egg to hold the mixture loosely together.

Stuff the neck end of the goose, pressing it in as far as it will go. Tuck the neck flap under and secure with a skewer if necessary.

Lay the goose on a wire rack in the roasting tin. Season well.

Roast at 210°C/425°F/gas mark 7 for 30 minutes. Reduce the oven temperature to 180°C/350°F/gas mark 4 and give the goose about another 3¼ hours. Test by pressing a skewer into the thickest part of the leg – the juices should run clear.

Prune and Apple Stuffing

Ingredients:

2 onions, finely chopped

2 tbsp unsalted butter

1 lb (450g) prunes, soaked in Armagnac, brandy or Calvados, then chopped

3 oz (250g) 'no need to soak' apricots, chopped

4 apples, peeled and diced

4 oz (100g) brown breadcrumbs

4 oz (100g) finely chopped walnuts

Method:

Saute the onion in butter and then add the rest of the ingredients.

Press the stuffing into a shallow baking dish and dot with extra butter.

Cover and bake at 180°C/350°F/gas mark 4 for 30-40 minutes.

programme 7 — Mulled Wine

Ingredients:

- 2-3 cinnamon sticks
- 6-8 cloves
- thinly pared rind 1 orange
- thinly pared rind 1 lemon
- 2 bottles full bodied red wine
- 6 tbsp unrefined demerara sugar or soft brown sugar
- grated nutmeg
- 2 fl oz (50ml) dark rum or brandy

Method

There is one simple rule when making hot mulled drinks — NEVER LET THEM BOIL.

Place the cinnamon, spices and fruit rinds in a basin. Just cover with boiling water and leave to stand for 15 minutes. Strain and reserve the liquid.

Pour the red wine into a large saucepan and add the spiced liquid and sugar. Heat through gently.

Add the brandy or rum and heat again.

Pour into suitable glasses using a jug. Decorate the glasses with orange slices.

Braised Red Cabbage

Ingredients:

- 1 oz (25g) butter
- 1 onion, thinly sliced
- 1½ lb (675g) red cabbage, thinly shredded
- 2 tbsp soft brown sugar
- 2 tbsp red wine vinegar
- ¼ pint (150ml) red wine
- 8 oz (225g) cranberries

Method:

Melt the butter in a large pan and cook the onion until soft but not brown.

Add the red cabbage, stir well. Cook for 5 minutes then add the sugar, red wine vinegar and red wine.

Bring to the boil then reduce the heat and cover. Cook for approximately 1 hour until the mixture is pulpy and well reduced.

Add the cranberries and cook for another 10 minutes.

Season, and serve with the roast goose.

programme **7** — # *Egg Nog*

Ingredients:

2 egg yolks
1 tbsp caster sugar
4 tbsp whipping cream
2 egg whites
4 tbsp dark rum
4 tbsp Cognac or apple brandy (Calvados)
chopped ice
nutmeg (optional)
mint (optional)

Method:

Beat together the two egg yolks and sugar.

Whip up the cream and stir gently into the egg yolks. Whisk one egg white until stiff and combine with egg yolks.

Add the rum and brandy.

Add chopped ice and pour the mixture into a cocktail shaker (any jar with a tight-fitting lid will do).

Shake vigorously.

Pour into glasses. Decorate with egg white (already beaten into stiff peaks), grated nutmeg and mint.

Cheers! Restaurateurs Robert Carrier (left) and Brian Turner celebrate Christmas with an egg nog.

Chocolate, Rum and Chestnut Roulade

Ingredients:

6 oz (175g) plain chocolate, broken into pieces
2 tbsp rum
5 eggs, separated
6 oz (175g) caster sugar
¼ pint (150ml) double cream
4 tbsp sweetened chestnut purée
icing sugar

Method:

Line a 12"x9" Swiss roll tin with non-stick paper.

Melt the chocolate in a bowl over a pan of simmering water or in a microwave.

In a separate bowl combine the egg yolk and caster sugar.

Beat with an electric or rotary whisk until the mixture has doubled in volume.

Fold in the melted chocolate.

Whisk the egg whites in a clean grease-free bowl until stiff but not dry.

Fold into the chocolate mixture and level the surface.

Bake for 20 minutes at 180°C/350°F/gas mark 4 or until the surface is firm to the touch.

Cover with a sheet of non-stick paper then a damp tea towel and leave to cool for several hours or overnight.

Turn out the roulade onto another sheet of non-stick paper. Peel off the lining paper.

Whip the cream until floppy. Fold the rum into the chestnut purée and then combine the filling ingredients together.

Spread the cream and chestnut filling over the roulade then roll up from the long end using the paper as a guide.

NB Do not worry if the roulade cracks – it is meant to!

Dust with icing sugar and don't even think about calories – it's Christmas!

programme 7 — Roast Beef and Yorkshire Pudding

Ingredients:

1 sirloin of beef weighing 6-8 lb (2.7-3.6kg) or use a fore rib joint
seasoning

The wing or prime rib is one of the largest and most expensive but without doubt one of the best roasting joints. The proportions of lean meat, and fat, will produce a majestic roast – but unless you are feeding a very large party you may be better off with a sirloin joint. You can also use a fore rib or best rib – another traditional roasting joint.

Ingredients for the Yorkshire Puddings:

plain flour
eggs
milk and water
measuring jug or mug to measure ingredients by volume – do not weigh

Method:

Pre-heat the oven to 220°C/425°F/gas mark 7.

Trim off any surplus fat and lay the beef skin side up in a roasting tin. Season well.

Place in the oven and allow approximately 15 minutes per pound for rare beef.

Method:

Tip the flour into the measuring jug and then place in a mixing bowl.

Break sufficient eggs into the jug to fill to the top. Place these in the mixing bowl.

Fill the jug or container with equal quantities of milk and water. Add to the mixing bowl. Season.

Whisk the batter really well – it should be the consistency of single cream.

Heat one tablespoon of oil in a 6" Yorkshire pudding tin or use a tray of individual ones – the fat or oil should produce a blue haze before you pour the batter in.

Quickly pour enough batter into the tins to come half way up.

Place in a hot oven 220°C/425°F/gas mark 7 for approximately half an hour or until the pudding is well risen and golden brown.

 # Honey and Chilli Roast Parsnips

Ingredients:

1 lb (450g) peeled and quartered parsnips
2 green chillies, diced and seeded
2 red chillies, diced and seeded
4 tbsp runny honey
2 tbsp soy sauce

Method:

Prepare the parsnips. Quarter and par-boil for 10 minutes.

Finely dice the green and red chilli. NB do take care not to touch your eyes when you have prepared chillies. It is best to remove the seeds under running water.

Lay the blanched parsnips in a flat dish.

Sprinkle with the diced chilli.

In a basin mix together the honey and soy sauce.

Spoon over the parsnips and chillies.

Bake at 200°C/400°F/gas mark 6 for 30 minutes. Serve with the beef and Yorkshire puddings.

programme 7 — *Pesto and Prawn Nibbles*

Ingredients:

- 8 oz (225g) puff pastry or flaky pastry
- 24 king prawns, raw or cooked
- 2 oz (50g) butter
- 1 clove of garlic, crushed
- 4 tsp pesto sauce
- a little grated lemon rind
- seasoning
- 2 oz (50g) chopped pine nuts
- beaten egg

Method:

Roll the pastry out thinly. Cut out squares approximately 4" then cut into triangles.

Melt the butter in a frying pan.

Roughly chop the prawns and sauté with the garlic, pesto, pine nuts and lemon rind for about 4-5 minutes.

Cool the mixture.

Spoon a little mixture onto each triangle of pastry.

Roll up from the longer end leaving the pointed end on top.

Brush with beaten egg.

Bake at 200°C/400°F/gas mark 6 for 5-10 minutes until golden brown. Serve with mulled wine.

Sausage and Bacon Bites

Ingredients:

- 1 lb (450g) cocktail sausages
- ½ lb (225g) streaky bacon
- 2 tbsp mustard – ready prepared
- 4 oz (125g) sliced Cheddar cheese

Method:

Pan-fry the cocktail sausages for 4-5 minutes until golden brown. Cool.

Make a slit along each sausage. Spread a little mustard in the sausage. Insert a baton of cheese.

Wrap the sausage and cheese with streaky bacon.

Place the bacon bites under a hot grill and cook until the bacon is golden brown but not too crispy.

Serve hot or cold with mulled wine.

Pumpkin Risotto

Ingredients:

8 oz (225g) Arborio or risotto rice

2 pints (1.2 litres) hot vegetable stock

8 oz (225g) diced pumpkin or use any variety of squash (eg acorn, gem, butternut) including courgette. Alternatively use mushrooms and bacon, prawns, crabs etc

4 oz (100g) unsalted butter

2 onions, diced

1-2 tbsp finely grated Parmesan

4 tbsp freshly chopped parsley

Parmesan flakes

2-3 tbsp cream (optional)

Method:

Bring the stock to a simmer and have a ladle at hand.

Melt the butter and add the onion and cook for 3-4 minutes without browning.

As the onion begins to soften add the rice and cook for 2-3 minutes.

Add 2-3 ladles of hot stock and stir frequently. The hot stock will steam and begin to evaporate. Add the pumpkin.

Continue to add the stock a little at a time until the rice is tender and the pumpkin is cooked. This takes approximately 20 minutes. (Don't cover the pan – allowing the stock to evaporate gives a better consistency to the risotto).

Stir in the grated Parmesan and a little extra butter – and cream if desired. Stir in the chopped parsley.

Spoon the risotto into individual bowls and scatter with flakes of Parmesan. A trickle of olive oil gives a nice touch.

Serve with granary bread.

Roast Pheasant with Apples and Calvados

Ingredients:

1 brace pheasant

oil and butter

2 bay leaves or sprig fresh thyme

streaky bacon

for the sauce:

2 oz (50g) unsalted butter

2 shallots, finely chopped

2 eating apples, chopped

1 glass Calvados or chicken stock

¼ pint (150ml) double cream

seasoning

Pheasant is very lean, so it helps to protect it during cooking. Streaky bacon strips are good for this purpose. You could also smear the pheasant with butter.

Roasting the birds breast side down also helps to keep them moist because the juices flow into the breasts rather than towards the back.

Method:

Lightly season the birds and heat a little oil and butter in a large pan. Brown the birds quickly on all sides.

Transfer to a roasting dish, breast side down, and insert a couple of bay leaves or a sprig of fresh thyme in the cavity of the bird.

Lay a few pieces of bacon over the birds.

Cook the pheasant according to weight but allow 20 minutes per pound only in a very hot oven – 220°C/425°F/gas mark 7.

Cover with foil whilst you make the sauce.

Melt the butter in a shallow pan and soften the shallots.

Stir in the apple pieces, add the Calvados and bring to the boil. At this stage you can flambé the Calvados.

When the flames have died away stir in the cream and whisk. Cook the sauce for a few minutes to reduce slightly. Season and keep warm.

Joint the pheasant and arrange on a platter. Pour the sauce over.

Petti di Pollo alla Yolanda

guest recipe from The French Partridge restaurant, Horton

Ingredients:

4 chicken breasts (skinless)

2 eggs, beaten

8 oz (225g) grated cheese (Cheddar and fresh Parmesan)

butter and sunflower oil

16 medium size fresh asparagus spears (cooked)

Method:

Slightly flatten the chicken breasts and spread with a batter made with the eggs and some of the cheese and milled white pepper.

Heat a non-stick pan with a little oil and fry the chicken on each side until golden.

Arrange the asparagus on the chicken. Sprinkle with a little more cheese.

Add a knob of butter.

Cover with a tight-fitting lid.

Place pan over a gentle heat to finish cooking and melt cheese.

Mushrooms on the Wild Side

Ingredients:

1 lb (450g) mushrooms – you can use a selection you have gathered, but you can now get packs of wild mushrooms from most supermarkets – or just use button or field mushrooms
¼ pint (150ml) white wine
¼ pint (150ml) double cream
2 tbsp snipped chives
¼ pint (150ml) white sauce
2 oz (50g) unsalted butter
seasoning

Method:

Roughly chop the mushrooms. Place the wine in a saucepan.

Add the mushrooms and poach gently, stirring occasionally. Season.

Make the white sauce, using ½ oz (15g) butter; ½ oz (15g) plain flour; and ¼ pint (150ml) milk. Melt the butter, stir in the flour, cook for 1 minute then add the milk slowly, stirring constantly. Bring to the boil. Season.

Stir the poached mushrooms into the sauce, followed by the cream. Heat until bubbling. Add a knob or two of butter to give the sauce a glossy finish. Stir in the chives.

Pile the mushroom sauce on granary toast or serve on puff pastry discs.

More Mushrooms

Ingredients:
8 oz (225g) wild or other mushrooms
2 fat cloves garlic, crushed
2 tbsp chopped parsley
seasoning
2 oz (50g) unsalted butter

Method:
Melt the butter in a large frying pan.

Add the crushed garlic. Cook for 1-2 minutes.

Add the mushrooms and stir quickly in the garlic butter until they begin to reduce.

Add the chopped parsley. Season with plenty of black pepper.

Serve on rounds of freshly buttered granary bread.

Wild Mushrooms

In general, fungi of all kinds favour damp habitats – woods and forests. Chanterelles and ceps are said to favour beech woods; field mushrooms grow best in meadows where cows and horses have grazed.

Most mushrooms can be found in the early autumn before the frosts arrive. You should always pick early in the morning before flies etc have had a chance to spoil them.

Important:
You should never pick any mushrooms from the wild unless you can positively identify them. Many of the edible varieties can easily be confused with inedible ones. If in doubt do **not** pick them.

If you are thinking of gathering wild mushrooms always take an expert with you or a reliable and very detailed guide book.

Braised Celery au Gratin

Ingredients:

6 celery sticks
1 large onion
carrots
salt and pepper
½ pint (300ml) dry cider

Method:

Chop onion and carrots into fine dice.

Fry them for a few minutes with a little oil in a heavy-bottomed saucepan.

Cut celery into large diamond-shaped chunks and add to the saucepan. Season with salt.

Pour over the dry cider (or vegetable stock). Cover with a lid and cook for around 30 minutes until the celery begins to go soft.

Meanwhile, make a plain white sauce with milk, flour, and butter.

Add a little of the celery cooking liquor, plus some double cream (optional) and 2 egg yolks. Stir well to remove any lumps.

After celery has been cooking for around 30 minutes transfer contents to roasting dish. Pour the white sauce over the top.

Sprinkle with a generous helping of white breadcrumbs and grated cheese.

Place in a moderate oven for another 20 minutes until golden and crispy on the top.

Celery and Apple Soup

Ingredients:

1 lb (450g) celery, washed and sliced
8 oz (225g) fresh tomatoes, deseeded and diced
8 oz (225g) red skinned apple, cored and diced
4 oz (100g) tiny pasta shapes (for the soup)
seasoning
1 small onion, diced
2 oz (50g) unsalted butter
2 pints (1.2 litres) chicken or vegetable stock
¼ pint (150ml) dry sherry
snipped chives for garnish

Method:

Melt the butter in a large saucepan, add the celery and onion and cook gently until the vegetables are softened but not brown.

Add the tomatoes, apples, sherry and stock. Season well.

Cover and bring to the boil then reduce the heat and simmer for 10-15 minutes.

Add the pasta shapes and cook for another 5 minutes or until the pasta is cooked. Check the seasoning again.

Serve in warm bowls with snipped chives scattered over. Accompany with crunchy croûtons or hunks of soda bread for a tasty lunchtime snack.

Sampling Celery Soup in Ely market.

An 'Offaly' Good Breakfast!

serves 4

Ingredients:

12 lambs' kidneys

2 oz (50g) butter

8 rashers smoked streaky bacon, cut into strips (lardons)

12 oz (350g) button mushrooms

1 level tbsp flour

10 fl oz (275ml) red wine

seasoning

Lambs' kidneys are at their best in spring and summer when the lamb is also at its best. Buy them encased in their own fat if you can. If you do buy frozen ones they really need a sauce to go with them to bring out their flavour.

Method:

First prepare the kidneys. Peel off the skins, cut in half and strip out the white cores. Half each piece again.

Melt the butter in a frying pan, add the bacon and cook until golden brown. Then add the mushrooms and continue to cook for 2-3 minutes.

Add the halved kidneys and toss with the bacon and mushrooms – they will change colour.

Sprinkle the flour into the pan to soak up the juices and stir well.

Pour in the red wine and stir continuously until the mixture thickens.

Cover and simmer for 10-15 minutes. Season.

Serve on rounds of toast or fried bread.

Chicken en Cocotte

Ingredients:

1 large chicken about 4 lb (1.8kg) in weight
4 plum tomatoes, not too ripe
1 tbsp fresh oregano or 2 tsp dried
4 tbsp fresh thyme or 2 tsp dried
4 tbsp extra virgin olive oil
seasoning
¼ pint (150ml) white wine
juice of 1 lemon
1 can of artichoke hearts in brine or oil
¼ pint (150ml) good stock
4 oz (100g) button mushrooms
3 oz (75g) unsalted butter
2 tbsp freshly chopped parsley
2 slices white bread, preferably a day old
olive oil

Method:

Quarter and de-seed the plum tomatoes. Lay in a flat dish.

Sprinkle with the chopped herbs, season generously and leave to marinate for 1 hour.

Gently ease the skin away from the chicken breast and push the marinated tomatoes under the skin.

Heat a little butter plus oil in a large flameproof casserole. Seal the chicken on all sides until lightly brown.

Meanwhile heat more butter and oil in a frying pan. Sauté the mushrooms. Place in casserole with chicken.

Add the white wine and lemon juice. Cover casserole and cook in the oven for approximately 1¼ hours.

Remove lid from casserole and pierce the chicken in the leg area – the juices should run clear. Remove chicken.

Add the artichokes and a little more lemon juice and the stock to the pan. Bring to the boil. Thicken if required.

In a separate frying pan heat a little oil, and fry cubes of white bread until golden brown.

Place the chicken in a suitable dish.

Pour the sauce over the chicken.

Sprinkle with the croûtons and the chopped parsley.

Pan-Fried Venison Steaks

Ingredients:

4 venison loin steaks
2 oz (50g) unsalted butter
4 red apples
1 lemon – juice only
8 oz (250g) cranberries
2 oz (50g) unrefined soft brown sugar
1 large onion, finely chopped
¼ pint (150ml) red wine
1 small Savoy cabbage
2 cloves of garlic, crushed
pinch of caraway seeds
seasoning

Method:

Season the venison steaks.

Melt the butter in a pan and pan-fry the venison steaks on each side for 3-4 minutes until they are lightly golden brown.

Meanwhile, make the apple baskets. Cut in half – remove core with a melon baller. Sprinkle with lemon juice to prevent them from browning.

In a small pan melt a little more butter and sprinkle in the brown sugar. Add the cranberries. Stir until the cranberries begin to soften – this will take 4-5 minutes.

Fill the apple baskets with the cranberry mixture and place in the oven – 180°C/350°F/gas mark 4 for 10-15 minutes.

Remove steaks from the frying pan and keep warm.

Add the chopped onions to the pan, cook gently but do not allow to colour.

Add the red wine to the pan – simmer and reduce the mixture by half.

Meanwhile finely shred the cabbage.

Place the butter and garlic in a heated frying pan and allow to cook for 2-3 minutes.

Add the sliced cabbage and caraway seeds if using. Toss the cabbage in the garlic butter until cooked through – about 5 minutes.

Remove apple baskets from the oven, place on a serving dish. Make a bed of cabbage alongside the apples. Slice the venison steaks – open out and place on top of the cabbage.

Pour the red wine sauce over and serve.

Salmon Niçoise

programme 10

Ingredients:

4 salmon filllets
1 oz (25g) unsalted butter
¼ pint (150ml) extra virgin olive oil
2 limes or 2 lemons
1 lb (450g) tomatoes – skinned and seeded
4 oz (100g) fine green beans
2 oz (50g) pitted black olives
2 tbsp snipped chives
2 tbsp shredded basil
4 oz (100g) sliced new potatoes (optional)

Method:

Lightly cook the beans until *al dente*.

In a separate pan cook the new potaotes if using.

Meanwhile, cook the salmon fillets on a greased griddle pan, or pan-fry in the butter until golden and just cooked. Keep warm.

In a separate pan, add the olive oil, rind and juice of the two lemons and limes. At this stage you could also add a dash or two of balsamic vinegar.

Heat the mixture gently, season, then add the diced tomato, green beans, potatoes, and olives.

Stir well then fold in the snipped chives and shredded basil.

Pile the warm salad in the centre of a plate. Arrange the salmon on top of the vegetables.

Spoon a little of the warm dressing around the salmon. Garnish with a sprig of basil.

programme 10 — Crêpes Suzette

Ingredients:

4 oz (125g) plain flour
pinch salt
1 egg, beaten
½ pint (300ml) milk
1 tbsp vegetable oil

for the orange sauce:

2 oz (50g) unsalted butter
2 oz (50g) caster sugar
grated rind and juice of 2 large oranges
grated rind and juice of 1 large lemon
2 tbsp Grand Marnier
2 tbsp brandy

Method:

Sift flour and salt into a bowl and make a well in the centre.

Add the egg and gradually add half the milk stirring constantly.

Add the oil and beat well until smooth. Add the remaining milk and leave to stand for 30 minutes.

Heat a 6" (15cm) omelette pan and add a few drops of oil. Pour in one tablespoon batter and tilt the pan to coat the bottom evenly.

Cook until the underside is brown and then toss and turn over to cook the other side for about 10 seconds.

Turn out onto a tea towel and cover with a disc of bakewell parchment. Continue to make pancakes with the remaining batter.

To make the orange sauce, melt the butter in the frying pan, add the sugar, orange rind and juice and heat until bubbling.

Dip each crêpe into the sauce, fold in quarters then place in a warm serving dish.

Add the Grand Marnier and brandy to the pan, heat gently and then ignite.

Pour the flaming liquid over the crêpes and serve immediately.

useful addresses

NORTH NORFOLK
- Richard and Julie Davies supply crabs from 7 Garden Street, Cromer, Norfolk. Telephone 01263 512727
- The Hoste Arms, The Green, Burnham Market, Norfolk. Telephone 01328 738257
- Humble Pie, The Market Place, Burnham Market, Norfolk. Telephone 01328 738581

PETERBOROUGH
- Tuxford & Tebbutt sell Stilton and other cheeses. Contact them at Thorpe End, Melton Mowbray, Leicestershire LE13 1RE. Telephone 01664 500555
- The Bell Hotel, Stilton, Peterborough, Northamptonshire. Telephone 01733 241066
- CAMRA, the Campaign for Real Ale, organised the Beer Festival. Their address is: 34 Alma Rd, St Albans, Hertfordshire AL1 3BN.

CAMBRIDGE
- Chivers Pick Your Own and Farm Shop, Impington, Cambridge. Telephone 01223 237799
- The Orchard Tea Garden, Mill Way, Grantchester, Cambridge CB3 9ND. Telephone 01223 845788

ESSEX
- Crapes Fruit Farm, Rectory Rd, Aldham, Colchester, Essex CO6 3RR. Telephone 01206 212375
- Linden Lady Chocolates, Walnut Tree Farm, Birch Rd, Copford. Telephone Paul Stockbridge on 01206 330240
- Colchester Oyster Fishery Ltd, Pyefleet Quay, North Farm, East Mersea. Telephone 01206 384141
- The Pier, Harwich. Telephone 01255 241212

SUFFOLK
- Shawsgate Vineyard, Badingham Rd, Framlingham, Suffolk IP13 9HZ. Telephone 01728 724060
- Neeve & Son Butchers, Curers & Smokers, 21 Cross Greeen, Debenham, Suffolk IP14 6RW. Telephone 01728 860240
- The Lighthouse, 77 High St, Aldeburgh, Suffolk IP15 5AU. Telephone 01728 453377

BRECKLAND/WEST NORFOLK
- Narborough Trout Farm, Narborough, King's Lynn, Norfolk PE32 1TE. Telephone 01760 338005
- Strattons Hotel, Stratton House, 4 Ash Close, Swaffham, Norfolk PE37 7NH. Telephone Vanessa and Les Scott on 01760 723845.
- Peele's Turkeys, Rookery Farm, Thuxton, Norwich NR9 4QJ. Telephone James Graham on 01362 850237
- Fiona Dickson (supplier of honey), Didlington Manor, Didlington, Thetford, Norfolk IP26 5AT. Telephone 01842 878673

NORTHAMPTONSHIRE
- Wakefield Farm Shop, Paulersbury, near Towcester, Northamptonshire. Telephone 01327 811493
- Pumpkins and Squashes, West View Farm, Brampton Lane, Chapel Brampton, Northamptonshire. Telephone 01604 843206
- Bruerne's Lock (restaurant), The Canalside, Stoke Bruerne, Towcester, Northamptonshire. Telephone 01604 863654
- French Partridge (restaurant), Horton, Northampton. Telephone David and Mary Partridge on 01604 870033
- Peter Jordan's Mushroom Forays, The Tasty Mushroom Partnership, Poppy Cottage, Station Rd, Burnham Market, Norfolk. Telephone 01328 738841
- Hind & Hart Hotel Boat Cruising, 7 Bramshill Gardens, London NW5 1JJ. Telephone 0171 272 0033

ELY/NEWMARKET
- The Chifney Restaurant, Tattersalls, Park Paddocks, Newmarket, Suffolk CB8 9AU. Telephone 01638 666166
- The Comfort Café, Fourwentways Roundabout, Abington, Cambridge CB1 6AP. Telephone 01223 837891
- Twenty Two (restaurant), 22 Chesterton Rd, Cambridge CB4 3AX. Telephone 01223 351880

WOBURN/OLNEY
- Paris House (restaurant), Woburn Park, Woburn MK17 9QP. Telephone 01525 290692
- The Carrington Arms, Cranfield Rd, Moulsoe, near Milton Keynes MK16 0HB. Telephone 01908 218050
- Flitwick Manor, Church Rd, Flitwick, Bedfordshire MK45 1AE. Tel 01525 712242
- Sutherland Game, c/o Millbrook Golf Club, Millbrook, near Woburn, Bedfordshire. Telephone 01525 840520

notes